RIBBL

SHORT · SCENIC · WALKS

PAUL HANNON

HILLSIDE PUBLICATIONS
20 Wheathead Crescent
Keighley
West Yorkshire
BD22 6LX

First Published 2010

© Paul Hannon 2010

ISBN 978 1 907626 03 6

The sketch maps are based on 1947 OS one-inch maps and earlier OS six-inch maps

Cover illustration: River Ribble at Mitton Bridge
Back cover: On Bradford Fell
Page 1: River Ribble at Marles Wood, Ribchester
(Paul Hannon/Hillslides Picture Library)

Printed by Steffprint
Unit 5, Keighley Industrial Park
Royd Ings Avenue
Keighley
West Yorkshire
BD21 4DZ

CONTENTS

INTRODUCTION

After having made a major contribution to the Yorkshire Dales landscape the Ribble moves on to become Lancashire's finest river on its way to the sea beyond Preston. The term Ribble Valley is commonly appended to its largest section both up- and down-stream of Clitheroe, a bustling market town watched over by a Norman keep on its limestone knoll. Open to visitors, the climb to the top is rewarded with a superb Ribble Valley prospect: within the grounds a museum exhibits much of local interest.

Throughout most of this area the Ribble is over-looked by the brooding mass of Pendle Hill, with delightful villages such as Downham and Pendleton at its feet. History abounds at the monastic sites of Whalley and Sawley, while many fine old houses with mullioned windows and weathered datestones reach back through the centuries. Today the Ribble Valley's string of villages is firmly on the visitor's trail, and the likes of Waddington and Bolton-by-Bowland are as fair as any in the land.

Swanside Bridge, Downham

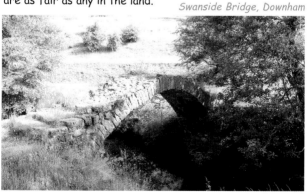

Richly varied walking alternates lush riverbanks with open country: Waddington and Longridge Fells as well as Pendle's western flank look down on the Ribble, which is supported by the lower reaches of the rivers Hodder and Calder. These walks touch the fringes of adjacent Bowland: while the Forest of Bowland Area of Outstanding Natural Beauty may be based on that upland mass to the west, its boundaries absorb many surrounding villages, and a detached section takes in the environs of Pendle Hill. Both Pendle and Bowland are covered by companion guides in this series.

The majority of walks are on rights of way with no access restrictions. A couple make use of 'Right to Roam' to cross Open Country: these areas can be closed for up to 28 days each year subject to advance notice, though the small sections in these walks are unlikely to be affected. Note that most walks can also be accessed by public transport. Whilst the route description should be sufficient to guide you around each walk, a map is recommended for greater information: Ordnance Survey 1:25,000 scale maps give the finest detail, and Explorers OL41 and 287 cover all the walks.

USEFUL INFORMATION

·Lancashire Countryside Service (01772-534709)
·Clitheroe Tourist Information (01200-425566)
·Open Access (0845-100 3298)
www.countrysideaccess.gov.uk
·Traveline - public transport information (0870-6082608)

Cattle at a dewpond above Ribchester

RIBBLE VALLEY

20 Short Scenic Walks

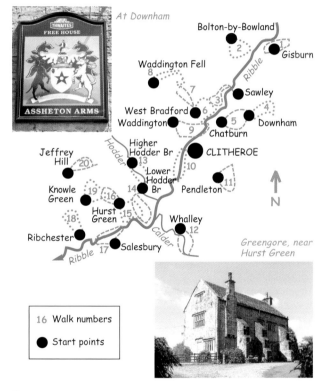

At Downham

ASSHETON ARMS
THWAITES
FREE HOUSE

Bolton-by-Bowland
2
1
Gisburn
Ribble

Waddington Fell
8
7
3
Sawley
West Bradford
6
4
Waddington
5
Downham
9
Chatburn
Higher
Hodder Br
13
CLITHEROE
Jeffrey
Hill
20
Hodder
Lower
Hodder
10
Knowle
Green
19
16
14
Br
Pendleton
11
Hurst
15
Green
18
Whalley
Ribchester
12
17
Salesbury
Ribble
Calder

N

Greengore, near
Hurst Green

| 16 | Walk numbers |
| ● | Start points |

6

A RECORD OF YOUR WALKS

WALK	DATE	NOTES
1		
2		
3		
4		
5		
6		
7		
8		
9		
10		
11		
12		
13		
14		
15		
16		
17		
18		
19		
20		

3^{1}2 miles from Gisburn

Parkland and a lively beck on the edge of an old village

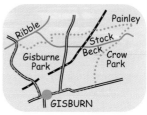

Start Village centre (GR: 830488), parking on Mill Lane by auction mart
Map OS Explorer OL21, South Pennines or Explorer OL41, Forest of Bowland & Ribblesdale

Gisburn is a busy street village astride the A59. Centrepiece is the church of St Mary the Virgin, with its Norman tower and nave stonework from Sawley Abbey. It contains memorials to the Listers of Gisburne Park (later the Lords Ribblesdale). A fine building in the centre is Cromwell House, the former Ribblesdale Arms, dating from 1635 and with an inscription on its three-storey porch. There is a tearoom, two restaurants, a Post office/store, a garage store and the last surviving pub, the White Bull. From the church head west on the main street, and turn right along Mill Lane past the auction mart and WC. As the Blackburn-Hellifield railway line is bridged, along to the right Gisburn Tunnel's castellated entrances are evidence of Lord Ribblesdale's success in not having his parkland spoiled by the railway. Leaving the village, the road affords sweeping views over the Ribble Valley to Pendle Hill.

The road descends into woodland at Gisburn Bridge. Two main arches span the broad Ribble flowing through richly wooded surrounds - your only sighting of the river. Alongside is an old house sporting mullioned windows - note the tablet on the side. Don't cross the bridge, but double back to the left of the house and up a drive climbing through trees. Head past the house above, but as a branch runs on to Gisburne Park, swing right with the main drive. Remain on this, with the big house of Gisburne Park over to the left. The impressive nine bay front dates from around 1750, and was the former residence of Lord Ribblesdale: the first Lord is remembered for planting a million oaks by the Ribble. The house currently operates as a hospital. On joining its drive, your way crosses straight over and down through trees to an arched bridge on Stock Beck. As it runs along to a house, keep left on the track outside its grounds, doubling steeply back up the wooded bank. Emerging, it runs pleasantly along to meet the A682 Hellifield road.

Cross to a gate opposite and head across the pasture with a tiny stream. Where it runs underground, cross at a bridle-gate and aim for the far corner of the field. Here is a previously unseen underpass beneath the railway. At the other side, advance a few yards with the fence then take a gate in it. Follow it down a little, then bear left with another fence to a gate at the far end. Over to the right is Weets Hill, with Pendle Hill further back. Ahead, an old grassy way makes straight for Painley Farm. From the gate into its confines pass above the first barns, then turn down a yard to approach the house: now go right on a short track to a gate beneath those first barns. Emerging into a field slant down the bank to meet Stock Beck again, a lovely setting for a short stroll downstream to a footbridge. Across, a thin path points the way up the bank towards Crow Park just ahead, with a nice view back over the valley. From a gate pass through the farmyard, out past the house and along its surfaced, hedgerowed drive to meet the A59. Turn right on its capacious verge to re-enter the village.

Gisburn church

*3¹4 miles from
Bolton-by-Bowland*

**Gentle rambling on the
edge of a lovely village**

Start Village centre
(GR: 785494), car park
Map OS Explorer OL41, Forest of Bowland & Ribblesdale

Bolton-by-Bowland is a very attractive village boasting two greens, the smaller one with remains of a medieval cross and old stocks. Here is the Coach & Horses pub, shop/tearoom and WCs. St Peter & St Paul's 15th century church tower is a splendid edifice of a style unfamiliar to these parts. The church itself was rebuilt in 1852, but contains much older interest. In particular seek out the remarkable 1460s memorial to Sir Ralph Pudsay: 10ft long, it bears portraits of himself, 3 wives and 25 children carved in low relief. There is also a brass of Henry Pudsay (1509) and wife, while a 16th century font bears a more recent 'Mouseman' cover.

From the centre head east on the main street past the church to the large green. Keep on past the school and up the road rising out of the village. On a bend at a driveway at Cow House Hill, take the adjacent kissing-gate and head diagonally across the field: a scant line of trees initially points the way to a gate ahead. Slant gently right up the field to find a kissing-gate on the brow alongside the edge of a wood. Head down the fenceside towards the farmstead at Fooden. A kissing-gate sends you down a small enclosure to a gate into the heart of the hamlet. On the left is a lovely cottage, and lower down the yard is 17th century Fooden Hall, with a two-storey gabled porch and mullioned windows.

Opposite the cottage turn right between barns to a small gate in the corner, and bear right across a small enclosure to the first of several kissing-gates. Advance along the field bottom on a part-sunken green way, in the next field running atop a wooded bank falling steeply to the Ribble Gorge. Though screened by trees the river is heard below. At the next you emerge into open pasture above the gorge, running an enjoyable enclosed way between fences. Ignoring a cross-track, your thin path drops gently down to the very end, well beneath the buildings of Scott Laithe. From a kissing-gate and plank bridge cross a large, sloping pasture to the next kissing-gate, with a barn at the site of Bolton Hall in view ahead. Keep straight on to a gate in the wall in front and turn right along the track, dropping down to the edge of the houses. For more than four centuries Bolton Hall was home to the Pudsay family, but even its 1806 replacement was demolished in the 1960s.

Turn right on the drive: after crossing the cattle-grid into Bolton Park, turn left down a grass track outside the grounds. It drops through a couple of gates and on to a footbridge and setted ford on Skirden Beck. Across, resume on a track upstream, quickly rising away to some gates. Through a kissing-gate advance just a little further on the track, and from a kissing-gate on the right cross towards the bank above the beck. Keep on to a corner stile, then follow a headland path outside trees along the ploughed field edge. At the end it swings left away from the trees. Quickly take a stile in the hedge and rise left up a welcoming sheep pasture, merging with a fence. On the brow, across to the right is an old cross base. Drop with the fence to a wall-stile, meeting a drive which is followed left to Skirden Bridge on the edge of the village.

Bolton Park

4¹⁄4 miles from Sawley

Open views and a delightful riverside between two villages

Start Village centre (GR: 776465), roadside parking
Map OS Explorer OL41, Forest of Bowland & Ribblesdale

Sawley is a lovely village best known for Salley (old name) Abbey, founded by Cistercian monks in 1147. Small in scale and in the shadow of nearby Whalley Abbey, it suffered on more than one occasion from marauding Scots. The remains are in the care of English Heritage and open to the public. A lovely scene sees dabbling ducks on the green by the Spread Eagle pub, from where take the road downstream the short way to Sawley Bridge. The Ribble flows wide beneath its fine arches, while Penyghent and Fountains Fell are seen far to the north. Just over the bridge is a road junction. Turn briefly left, then sharp right along a short drive to the Friends' Meeting House: this Quaker establishment dates from 1777.

Two paths head away: take the left one, through a gate and winding up the bank behind the meeting house. It then rises faintly up a small wooded clough to emerge via a stile at the top. Continue up to join a driveway and follow it left to a junction with an access road. Big views look across the valley to Pendle Hill. Turn up this to the various dwellings at High House Farm. Keep on the main drive to enter the farmyard at the end, passing right of the white farmhouse to a gate into a small open area. Straight across are twin stiles in a hedge, then bear right to a gate at the field corner. Continue away along a hedgeside, reaching a gate/stile just short of the end. Bear right to cross a reedy trickle in the field centre, then advance on to the tapering corner. Over the stile rise gently to a gate/stile into the terminus of a green lane. Follow its broad, hedgerowed course up to join a driveway at two houses on the brow. Simply follow this away as it drops towards Grindleton.

At a Methodist Free Church of 1862 on the village edge you could drop left down the initially rough Back Lane to the through road, or keep straight on to the parallel main street just ahead.

Turn left down the main street, a lengthy descent past attractive corners. Both the Duke of York and the Buck Inn are set around a junction at the bottom: here turn right to drop down out of the village. Keep left at a junction to approach Grindleton Bridge. Just before it take a gate on the left to join the riverbank for a lovely stroll upstream, some sections having succumbed to recent erosion. Pendle Hill is straight ahead as you set off. A loop opposite the sewage works is short-cut on an embankment, soon closing in on the river again until a stile puts you back on the very bank. Further, just beyond a confluence the embankment ends, and a stile marks the end of this section. Bear left to a nearby stile near an outer corner, and bear right across the larger field to a ladder-stile on the wall at the far end. Though the head of a grassy lane is on the left, rise up the fieldside with a tree-lined stream to a stile at the top, then up a further field to a wall-stile onto a road. Turn right along the road past Bowland High School, soon dropping to a nice corner with woods, cottages and the river returning. From a stile on the right cross to another to rejoin the bank for the short stroll upstream back to Sawley Bridge.

Sawley Abbey

3³⁄4 miles from Downham

A charming ramble by beck-side and delectable pastures

Start Village centre
(GR: 785442), car park
Map OS Explorer OL21, South Pennines (or OL41)

Downham is a lovely village, its street climbing to St Leonard's church with 15th century tower: inside are monuments to the Assheton family whose arms adorn the pub across the road. The original Downham Hall was built by the Asshetons in Elizabethan times, though today's largely dates from 1835. Also at the top of the street is the Post office/café, while ducks dabble in the stream at the bottom overlooked by 16th century Old Well Hall. There is an information room/WCs at the car park. From the bridge climb the road towards the church. Above the pub turn right on a short drive, and at the end take a bridle-gate on the left. Ascend a short fieldside to a three-slab stile with modern kissing-gate, then rise to the modest brow of Downham Green. A clear day reveals a fine prospect up the valley to the peaks of the Yorkshire Dales, where Ingleborough and Penyghent grab attention.

Though a path goes straight on, your way slants gently down to the right. Through a steeper drop aim for some limestone knolls to the right. Approaching them, the base of an old cross is encountered, its socket distinct in what initially seems an isolated boulder. In front of the main tree-topped outcrop, descend left past smaller ones to a gate in a hedge. On the other side a drive leads right to Downham Mill in its idyllic setting. Now a private dwelling, the arch of this former corn mill's undershot waterwheel hole is prominent. Pass right of the house and out via a stile at the rear, where a grass track heads away past the old millpond.

The track heads away along the valley floor, through a kissing-gate and on to a footbridge on Twiston Beck. Cross and resume upstream, through a gate from where an intermittent path runs the length of this beckside pasture to a plank bridge and stile at a sidestream at the far end. Go right on a short boardwalk, and a delightful path heads away with the beck to a footbridge on Ings Beck close by its confluence with Twiston Beck. Here bear right, with Twiston Beck below and Pendle Hill looming ahead. Ignoring a footbridge down to the right, this lovely section leads through stiles and gates near meandering Twiston Beck to a barn grouping at Twiston Mill: a wall-stile alongside puts you onto a back road.

Go briefly right until it bridges the beck, and instead take a small gate on the left by the former mill dam. A briefly enclosed path emerges into a field, continuing a little further to a footbridge on the beck. Across, double back briefly then rise with an old hedgerow. From a gate/stile at the top head away with a hedge to meet a track at the end. Go left on its briefly enclosed course then turn right along the fieldside. Through a gate/stile at the end a track re-forms, and this brow is a splendid viewpoint. The fieldside track drops down to a former quarry: from a wall-stile on the right head away towards New Close Farm, but before the field end take a kissing-gate on the left. Head away with a hedge, and when this drops away advance on to a footbridge at the end. Now bear right across a large field to a stile in a tiny section of wall opposite. Cross the field corner to an identical set-up on your right, then to a gate/stile just ahead. Now bear right across to Downham Beck, which leads pleasantly down past a spring to enter the village.

Pendle from Downham

4 miles from Chatburn

Superb footpaths lead to and from a classic village beneath Pendle Hill

Start Village centre (GR: 769441), roadside parking

Map OS Explorer OL41, Forest of Bowland & Ribblesdale

Chatburn is a bright village with pubs, shops, the renowned Hudsons Ice Cream and a tall-spired church. Leave by the Downham road rising out of the village to bridge the A59 in its deep cutting: Pendle Hill is ahead, while Penyghent rises far to the left. Immediately across take a gate on the left and another behind it, and a track drops gently away. Keep straight on to a gate at the start of a long-running path enclosed by greenery. Bridging the railway it resumes as before, ultimately emerging into a field. Advance towards a barn ahead, deflected round its right side by gates to continue with a wall. From a kissing-gate drop by a hedge to a footbridge on a tiny stream. Across, the path crosses an unkempt pasture to the far corner. While your onward route is right, first step over the wall-stile below to visit Swanside Bridge, an old packhorse bridge with a graceful arch in a charming wooded dean (illustrated on page 4).

Back at the stile ascend a path outside the wood, turning left at the top to a railway underpass. Now bear right up the field to a gate above, then follow a wall up to a gate onto a road. Go right to a stile on the left, then bear right up the pasture of Downham Green to an ascending wall. Follow this over the brow to approach Downham, and drop down with the wall to a three-slab stile with kissing-gate. Descend a fieldside to a bridle-gate, then go right on a short drive to emerge at the top of the village. For a note on Downham see page 14. From the bridge at the bottom of the village turn right on a side road to the car park entrance. Between road and entrance, turn up a short drive to a couple of houses. Take a stile by a gate between them, and head off with a fence on the right, becoming briefly enclosed. From a gate at the end rise away outside a wood, with Pendle's whaleback rising majestically ahead.

At the end is a stile/kissing-gate. With the limestone knoll of Worsaw Hill ahead, bear left across a large field to a stile/gate in the far corner, and on a little further to another. Head away above a wall, now on the base of Worsaw Hill with increasing evidence of its limestone origins. Further on you pass above Worsaw End House, setting for the 1960s film 'Whistle Down the Wind'. Remain on the path winding around the base of the hill, with a glimpse of Clitheroe Castle ahead. The path rises gently away beneath a scrubby bank, then more openly to the brow of the hill. Amid limestone outcrops this brow is a lovely spot, and a fine viewpoint for Pendle, Longridge Fell, Bowland and even a glimpse of the top of Ingleborough.

The continuing path drops to a small gate, then slants down a scrubby bank of limestone and on to a corner wall-stile. Head away, dropping to a kissing-gate at the edge of the A59. Turn right on the parallel path until it rises to the road, which is crossed with care. Steps down the other side send an enclosed streamside path away to a driveway. Go left over the footbridge/ford then take a stile on the right. Descend an outer garden to a bridge back over the stream, then cross a drive to a tall gate to emerge onto an access road at the end of a long terrace. Go left past a Methodist church out onto the road, with the centre just down to the left.

Worsaw Hill

*3³⁄₄ miles
from West Bradford*

**A splendid stretch of the
Ribble linking two villages**

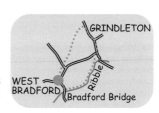

Start Village centre (GR: 742443), roadside parking:
village hall car park on Grindleton road
Map OS Explorer OL41, Forest of Bowland & Ribblesdale

West Bradford is an unassuming village featuring the
Three Millstones pub. From the T-junction in the centre take the
Clitheroe road branching off through the village, passing the old
pinfold and leaving the houses behind to reach the Ribble well
short of the three arches of Bradford Bridge. Here take a kissing-
gate on the left to join the river, through the edge of a garden and
over two footbridges to gain the bank proper. A superb riverbank
walk ensues, first enclosed then through a broad pasture before
being deflected by a fence to a gate in it. A clearer path runs past
a sewage works, and from its bridge regains the riverbank to
resume upstream. With unglamorous Grindleton Bridge in view
ahead, the path swings left to a small gate to rise as a snicket past
modern housing onto the West Bradford road.

Turn right and follow the road as it swings uphill towards
the centre of Grindleton. Both the Duke of York and the Buck Inn
are set around a junction: here turn left to climb the main street
proper, a lengthy pull punctuated by attractive corners. The climb
ends at a bus turning area at Top of Town: here go left through a
housing development to a kissing-gate into a field. Descend to a
footbridge on tree-lined Grindleton Brook, from where a short-
lived path slants up the other side. Advance above a tree-lined
sidestream which quickly fades to reveal a stile at the end.
Continue along a couple more fieldsides to a corner stile onto an
enclosed cart-track, Green Lane.

Just a few strides right take a stile on the left into a field, and slant right to a stile into the deep, wooded enclave of West Clough Brook. A path slants down to the floor to double back a few yards downstream to ford the little brook. Wooden steps aid a steep ascent of the opposite bank to a stile at the top. Back out into fields head away with a hedge above you, and when it turns off bear right to a stile in the facing hedge. Heading towards another stile in view ahead, don't use it but take a gate to its left. Past a red-brick outbuilding join a driveway, which leads out past the house to become surfaced at the next house, Marylebone Farm.

Advance a few steps further to a stile on the left before the next house. At the end of the garden a stile puts you into the field behind, and slant down towards the top end of a tree-lined stream, with stiles either side. In the next field follow a hedge away, and when it drops away continue to a stile ahead. Now cross to a bridle-gate in a hedge, dropping precariously onto a surfaced lane. From the stile opposite head away to another just ahead, then advance on above back gardens of West Bradford's suburbia. At the end a stile puts you on a drive at a couple of houses: follow it out and along a field bottom to a driveway above a farm. Drop left through the yard and back onto the road in West Bradford.

Bradford Bridge

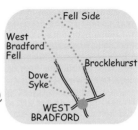

7 ——WEST BRADFORD FELL

4³⁄₄ miles
from West Bradford

A sustained, easy climb from pasture to fellside: big views

Start Village centre (GR: 742443), roadside parking: village hall car park on Grindleton road
Map OS Explorer OL41, Forest of Bowland & Ribblesdale

West Bradford is an unassuming village: pub and church help maintain a community atmosphere, while an old pinfold stands on the main street. At the head of the main street turn left on the Waddington road. At once note the old house of Pillings up to the right, with mullioned windows. Head past the Three Millstones pub and rising above the brook out of the village, take an unsigned byway right. This runs delightfully on above the brook, past an old burial ground. This sequestered spot adjoined a now demolished Methodist chapel of 1797. The track swings left up onto Eaves Hall Lane (later Moor Lane) beneath Eaves Hall Hotel. Go right a few strides and take a flight of steps left up into a garden edge. Cross to an old kissing-gate, and advance to cross a footbridge on a sidestream.

Follow a fence away as far as a stile in it, then ascend a large field to buildings above. Back over to the right is a glimpse of the red-brick facade of Eaves Hall, while high above is the mast on Waddington Fell. A stile left of the first house puts you onto a drive. From one opposite head past the side of the second house and bear left to a gate in the wall ahead. Ascend the next two fields to the contrasting houses at Dove Syke: a stile leads to a short enclosed way between them. On the drive, turn right as far as the end of trees on your left. As an access road comes in, take a stile on the left and slant to the top of a line of trees. From a stile/slab bridge resume the slant towards houses at Hancocks. A gate admits onto surfaced Moor Lane: turn uphill until it swings left to Seedalls Farm. Here take the gate in front and a rough track ascends to a barn.

Moor Lane now settles down as a part enclosed green track, gently gaining height. Soon you are entirely surrounded by open country of heather, bracken and moor grass. The track kinks right to quickly reach a second bend: instead of passing through the gate to continue up, pass through a gateway on the right and head off on another grassy wallside way. Through a gate it rises onto heather-clad moor, still with the now crumbling wall over a gentle brow: at 1000ft/305m on Sour Dock Hill this is the walk's summit. Path and wall drop down to the shell of the old farm at Fell Side. Without entering, turn right on the wallside green way. From the gate at the end advance a short way on a thinner trod, which then swings left to perform a dog-leg down this steeper pasture. It doubles sharply back through bracken to a gateway in the bottom corner. Drop straight down a reedy line to a marshy sidestream beneath a few trees. Across, slant right up the bank and cross to a gate where wall and fence meet. Head away with a wall, and a grassy track forms to lead down through fields to a gate onto a surfaced drive.

Continue down to the farm at Brocklehurst. Just beyond, take a gate/stile on the right into a large field just past the head of a wooded stream. Head away, parallel with the trees to a gate in a fence at a dry stream crossing. Now slant left, descending to a gate/stile: West Bradford's rooftops appear below. Slant down again, above a hedge corner. Continue through a scant line of hawthorns, and down to the foot of a drive just above a farm. This leads down through the yard and out onto the road at the head of the village.

Pendle Hill from under Fell Side

*3³⁄₄ miles from
Waddington Fell*

**A high altitude stride
over colourful moorland
slopes, with big views**

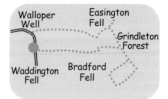

Walloper Well

Easington Fell

Grindleton Forest

Waddington Fell

Bradford Fell

Start **Road summit (GR: 719480), car park**
Map **OS Explorer OL41, Forest of Bowland & Ribblesdale**
Access **Open Access, see page 5**

At the outset keen eyes will see Ingleborough's summit appearing over your fell to the right. From the car park head north on the broad verge. The road soon descends to Walloper Well, where springs pour into roadside troughs. Here turn right onto the moor, down to cross the grassy wall of an old dam that served a smelting mill downstream. A trod rises beyond it to a shooting butt, just past which is a fine green track. Turn right, and at a major fork keep right to stride grandly across grassy moor. Reaching a ladder-stile on a wall, don't cross but take a thinner way rising left. This quickly eases to trace the wall along to the upper limit of Grindleton Forest. A boundary stone bears initials of Grindleton, West Bradford and Newton. Just beyond, a branch slants left to Easington Fell's cairn at 1299ft/396m. This great mass of fell you are tramping has any number of names depending on which part you're currently on: though Waddington Fell is widely used, Easington Fell narrowly claims its summit. The panorama stretches from Longridge Fell round via Beacon Fell, Bowland moors, Gragareth, Great Coum, Whernside, Ingleborough, Penyghent and Fountains Fell. Closer are Slaidburn, Stocks Reservoir and Gisburn Forest.

Back at the wall, retrace steps to the boundary stone, then step over the fence behind and a thin path descends by the old wall outside the forest fence. Dropping faintly through heather and two crumbled walls a bigger drop is revealed as the forest turns off left. With a boundary stone alongside, Pendle Hill rises across the valley. Drop with the fence to the head of an enclosed track by the forest edge: the path doubling back right will be your return route. Now descend the colourful track outside the forest, through a bridle-gate to a T-junction with another green lane from the right: you shall return here after a lower loop. Continue down outside the trees, and a forest road soon comes in with its harder surface. Through a gate continue a little further, then just above some scant ruins, pass through a gap in the crumbled wall on the right and head away on a green track. It quickly merges with another and runs on to a gate/stile in an old wall beyond a tiny stream crossing above a tiny plantation. Now bear left on a thin trod, merging with a long crumbled wall to cross to the shell of Fell Side.

Turn right on a grassy wallside way to a bridle-gate onto a walled green way. Turn right for a Roman-like march rising gently back to the forest-edge junction. Pass through the bridle-gate and return up the track to the corner where forest and moor meet. This time take the inviting path slanting left up through bracken to a prominent cairn on a knoll. The path continues to deflect left of a wall, dropping to a path crossroads at a pair of forlorn gateposts. Cross straight over on the path aiming directly for Waddington Fell's mast. The broad path crosses the moor to a gate/stile, becoming moister as the heather fades. Through it an improved green track makes a bee-line for the road summit in front of Waddington Fell Quarry. Turn right over the cattle-grid to finish.

On Easington Fell

4 miles
from Waddington

Ribble-side paths between
two fine bridges close
by a classic village

Start Village centre (GR:
728439), roadside parking;
playing fields car park signed on Bashall Eaves road
Map OS Explorer OL41, Forest of Bowland & Ribblesdale

Waddington is a showpiece village with a stream tinkling through. There are three pubs, tearoom, Post office/shop and WCs. St Helen's church retains its solid tower of 1501: inside are a 15th century font and medieval glass. The 'Hospital' is some delightfully laid out almshouses founded 300 years ago. Turn down the main street to the war memorial, noting Waddington Old Hall on the left. Restored a century ago, much of it dates back over 500 years: Henry VI spent time here after defeat at Hexham in 1464 during the Wars of the Roses. Here take a dark snicket heading away left to emerge into a field. From a stile ahead bear left to the far corner where a stile puts you onto a road on the village edge. Go right on the footway to the school. Ignoring a path through a gate opposite, advance a few yards further into the yard of Healings Farm.

Part way through take a path through trees on the left to emerge into a field. Cross to meet a track at the right-hand of two stiles, then bear right to a more obvious one in a fence. Advance to the edge of a colourful hollow, a path dropping to cross its part marshy floor to ascend a wooden stairway. The path then drops to a stile, with the cement works still as backdrop. Bear right across the field to another stile, then on again as a path re-forms to drop right through successive kissing-gates in undergrowth. Cross one last field corner to find yourself on the bank of the Ribble. Turn upstream to the waiting three arches of Bradford Bridge.

Across, take a stile on the right to resume downstream, a path faithfully tracing the river to a bend where you enter the trees of Cross Hill Quarry nature reserve. The path rises to join a level one, going right with it amid various examples of sculptures and mosaics. A little further you see the old quarry face set back to the left, exhibiting impressive tilted rock strata. Beyond, you are deflected up a bank to follow a hard, higher-level path through trees. Ignore any left branches and the way drops back towards the river to run on to a road at Brungerley Bridge. Well-screened WCs burrow into the hillside as you turn right to cross the impressive bridge. Built in the early 19th century, it is inscribed with townships and (real) counties it divides: 'Clitheroe, Lancashire; Waddington, Yorkshire'.

Across, rise briefly up the footway then take a gate on the left. An old drive heads away, quickly merging with the present one to go left to approach Waddow Hall. Dating from Tudor times, it has been substantially enlarged and serves as a girl guide centre. At a cattle-grid your path is deflected right up around the wall, dropping back down at the far end to an old carriageway. Follow this right, through parkland, with views to Longridge Fell and Parlick, with Waddington Fell re-appearing. At a gate onto a back road turn right to return to the centre of Waddington.

Waddington church

4¼ miles from Clitheroe

Easy Ribble-side walking between two old bridges

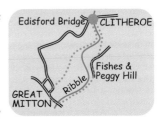

Start Edisford Bridge (GR: 726414), car park a mile out of town on B6243

Map OS Explorer OL41, Forest of Bowland & Ribblesdale

From the car park join the road where a path runs down to the riverside: on the opposite bank is the Edisford Bridge Inn. Cross the bridge and turn down the open bank: this opening section to the waterworks building mentioned is a landowner's concessionary path. Just short of the end of the area, take a stile on the right and follow a hedge away. Towards the corner, slant up to a stile in the top corner. Looking back, Pendle Hill rises beyond Clitheroe. Turn left on a track into woodland, emerging through a gate at the end. Join the riverbank to follow the Ribble downstream through a sweeping pasture, a delectable stroll seeming far from civilisation.

At the end a stile enters more natural woodland, and a little path climbs the bank to a stile. Ahead is the outline of Longridge Fell. Cross the field to the right of the waterworks building ahead, where a stile admits to a small enclosure. A gate in front puts you onto a junction of ways. To the right, a track comes down from the road, while your way takes a stile ahead, to the left. From it head left on the fieldside, to a stile at the end and then on by a tiny stream immersed in scrub. Keep straight on at a small confluence in a corner, now following a lesser stream towards the edge of a wood. Before reaching it, a bridge crosses the stream to a stile behind. Entering a vast field, bear steadily left to merge with the hedge. Pass a hollowed pool and keep on to a stile at the end, which admits to an old green way, Malkin Lane.

Turn right on this splendid enclosed way to join Church Lane in Great Mitton. Turn left, winding round to a junction in this tiny village. To the right is the Three Fishes pub, while on the corner is a tearoom. All Hallows church dates from the 14th century: inside is a pre-Reformation screen from Sawley Abbey, while the Shireburn chapel dates from 1594 and boasts numerous recumbent effigies. At the junction go left past the church and down the road to cross Mitton Bridge. The Ribble glides over rocky shelves downstream, while upstream it leads the eye to Pendle Hill. Note also, while crossing, the fine setting of Great Mitton's Old Hall and church.

At the bridge end is the Aspinall Arms, past which a kissing-gate points you upstream. The thin path follows a field edge to the far end, deflected by a wooded bank above the river. Through a stile a further fieldside leads to a kissing-gate and down to a foot-bridge on a stream, entering a large riverside pasture. Cross to a small waterworks building from where a grassy track leads upstream to a shapely aqueduct. Continue on a broad track to Shuttleworth Farm. Pass left of the buildings to follow the drive out past several houses (the curiously named Fishes and Peggy Hill) and continue upstream beneath a screened refuse site: here the river disappears. Your road heads straight on, absorbing the 'tip' road. Just past Mill House, a

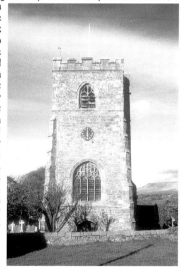

popular, unofficial path slips into the trees on the left, following the beck upstream to escape tip waggons. It rejoins the road at a stone-arched bridge. Just beyond, turn left on the drive towards Siddows Farm. At the early fork, go right a few yards then take a bridle-gate on the left, crossing a small field to a stile at the far corner. From here a path slants down to the river, which is followed upstream back to the starting point. A well-screened caravan site precedes the popular riverside picnic area with a miniature railway.

Great Mitton church

4 miles from Pendleton

A fine moorland stroll on the flanks of Pendle Hill

Start **Village centre (GR: 755396), car park**
Map **OS Explorer OL41,**
Forest of Bowland & Ribblesdale

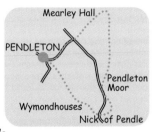

Pendleton is a hugely attractive linear village with a stream running through the centre, some fine houses and the Swan with Two Necks pub. On a tiny green is Fiddle Bridge, returned to the village in 2000 after 200 years absence. Take the road rising out of the village, which leaves by swinging left between the modest All Saints church (1847) and the old National School (1837, rebuilt 1870). With Pendle's moorland flanks above, it runs to a T-junction at a small green. Cross straight over to the farm road at Pendleton Hall, and head directly away, opening out to run through fields to approach Mearley Hall, an old house with mullioned windows.

Just short of the grounds, turn right up a fenceside to a gate/stile. An enclosed path rises by a tiny stream, emerging at the top to slant steadily right up the big sloping field. Continue up to a roofless barn at the top. Just behind it a ladder-stile puts you onto the foot of the open moor, and an intermittent trod bears off right through reedy terrain to approach Ashendean Clough. Views back over the Ribble Valley look to Longridge Fell, Beacon Fell, Parlick, Totridge and Waddington Fell. Drop towards the clough in line with a barn in the field opposite, angling in to find a footbridge between new plantings. Rise away with the wall, around to a gate in an intervening fence. Continue with the wall, rising slightly on a fading path across Pendleton Moor. Before the wall turns off, bear left on a trod rising still very gently, and maintain this course, crossing a better path then rising to meet another: bear right on this level path to join the Clitheroe-Sabden road at a parking area.

Turn left up the verge the short way to the Wellsprings pub-turned-restaurant. You might also watch the antics of those on the dry slopes of Pendle Ski Club. Turn left up a part-sunken way just yards short of the Wellsprings. This curves pleasantly up to the right to meet the wide Pendle ascent path on the broad moorland ridge. New views ahead reveal a long line of South Pennine moors. Clitheroe sits in the valley beneath a Bowland skyline, while far to the north are Ingleborough and Penyghent. Turn right for a brief, gentle descent to the road summit at the Nick of Pendle. At 985ft/300m this is a popular high-level start point for the ascent of Pendle Hill.

Cross with care and go briefly right to a wall-stile. A path slants down reedy pasture to merge with a wall opposite, dropping to a corner gate/stile. Behind, a track drops right with an old wall before continuing down to meet a solid wall below: just ahead is Wymondhouses. A short way down the wallside take a small gate in it, drop down to a part sunken way and slant left down to the side of the nearest house: this was an early Congregational church of 1667. Just behind is a small gate, with a wall-stile behind. Head directly away with an old hedge, and just short of the bottom take a gate on the right. Head away with a hedge to a gate/stile, then turn sharp left to resume the descent. Passing through a tree-line bear right to drop to a footbridge in the very far corner. Resume down the other side of the tree-lined stream, down a long, tapering field to the very bottom where a track forms to lead to a gate/stile by a house: through it the access road joins the road by the church at the head of the village.

Winter on Pendleton Moor

4¾ miles from Whalley

Richly varied rambling around the environs of the Calder

Start Town centre
(GR: 732361), car park
Map OS Explorer 287,
West Pennine Moors

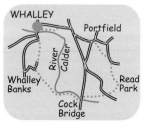

WHALLEY

Portfield

River Calder

Whalley
Banks

Read
Park

Cock
Bridge

Whalley is best known for its Cistercian abbey, entered through a gatehouse of 1480: finer still is a 14th century gatehouse over a road. St Mary & All Saints' church has a Norman doorway, 15th century stalls and three 9th-11th century crosses. Cross Whalley Bridge on the Calder at the south end of town, looking downstream to a massive 1850 red-brick viaduct. Turn sharp left up Moor Lane, climbing steeply through trees. At the first chance turn off left at a bend on a sunken bridleway climbing to a viewpoint above the river. The fork here is incidental, for path and bridleway rise parallel through a sliver of woodland to rejoin at the corner of Nab Wood. Go straight ahead on the sunken bridleway climbing to the top to meet an access road. Advance on this to houses just ahead, and straight on between them to a gate. A leafy little way runs to the larger grouping of houses at Whalley Banks.

Again keep straight on the access road until it climbs right, then take a short drive in front. Path and sunken bridleway run parallel here: take the path on the left to emerge via a kissing-gate into a field with big views. The thin path winds down to a tree-lined stream, and down to a kissing-gate/footbridge to meet another path. Turn down its enclosed course, at the end crossing the stream but quickly re-crossing a slab bridge. A path now contours another sloping pasture above the Calder. As it fades, advance to the end to drop left to approach Dean Brook. A path re-forms to cross a slab bridge to a kissing-gate into trees, and a path climbs steeply to run above the wooded riverbank. From a kissing-gate at the end the way runs more freely above the trees. A path then descends to the bank, crossing a sidestream for a superb, level stroll upstream. Across a footbridge on another stream you are deflected from the river by a part wooded bank, rising across the field to the A680. To the right is the Game Cock Inn.

Turn left to cross Cock Bridge, then right on a drive to a garden centre/tearoom. At its entrance take a stony track rising left beneath Cock Wood. Joining the A671, cross with care, and up past a lodge on the drive through Read Park. At Coppy Plantation turn left off the forking drive to a gate/stile, and a green track heads away outside the wood. Remain on this through several fields to descend to a road at Read Old Bridge, scene of a 1643 Civil War skirmish. Just up the other side take a farm drive left, but leave at the first chance by a stile on the right. Ascend directly to the brow, then on past a hollow to a stile ahead. Cross the next field to a gate/stile, bound for the houses at Portfield. Bear right to a stile across a smaller field then up another brow to a stile by the right-hand house, emerging onto a junction. Go briefly left then keep right down Portfield Road onto the A671: go right to cross at the traffic lights and take the side road to Whalley. At the 'Whalley' sign, take a path left to drop to the river. This leads downstream, and at a weir joins a rough lane back out onto the street.

By the Calder below Whalley Banks

*4 miles from
Higher Hodder Bridge*

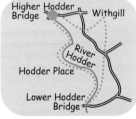

**Three fine bridges span the
delectable River Hodder**

*Start Higher Hodder Bridge
(GR: 697410),
parking at Clitheroe end*
Map OS Explorer OL41, Forest of Bowland & Ribblesdale

Begin by heading back up the road to Hodder Court, until 1994 the Hodder Bridge Hotel, its old sign survives. Turn right on a drive to several houses, ahead is Pendle Hill. Keep on to a stile/stile at the end, and head off by an old sunken way. Surrounded by delectable greenery high above a wooded curve of the unseen river, at the bottom corner are a stile and stone footbridge. Up the other side the old way curves away to the left, and part way up a stile transfers you into a field. Rise by the tree-lined stream to a stile onto a road. Longridge Fell's conifered slopes rise behind you.

Turn right a short way then go left on a drive through fields to Withgill Fold. Look left to see Longridge, Fair Snape and Waddington Fells. Keep right of all houses, then along an enclosed way past the last ones. Through a gate at the end go right up a paddock side to a gate onto a track. Go briefly right to a fork at a wood corner at Withgill Knoll. The true path angles off right here through undergrowth: it is easier to use the right fork outside the trees to a gate at the end, picking up the proper line by turning a short way right to a gate/stile in the wall. Now slant across the field to locate a stile in front of deeper trees opposite. There is a full prospect of Pendle Hill to the left. Head away with trees on the right, as they end bear left to a corner stile onto a road junction.

Advance less than 50 yards along the central option (B6243), and take a gate/stile on the right into a vast field. Head diagonally away past two oaks to a fence above the wooded bank of the Hodder. Go left with the fence to a corner stile, where a path runs through a belt of trees extending up from the bank. Over a stile at the end resume as before, ultimately dropping to a stile onto a road. Turn right to Lower Hodder Bridge: just downstream is the remarkable 16th century Cromwell's Bridge, so named as the historical figure came this way prior to the Battle of Preston in 1648.

Across the bridge a track heads upstream, unerringly round a big sweep of the Hodder. Through a gate at the end a broad path rises beneath a massive wall to approach Hodder Place. Once a junior school for Stonyhurst College, it is now flats. When the track turns left for it, keep straight on a broad path descending into woodland. Immediately after crossing a substantial stone bridge is a divergence of paths. Your way tackles the great flight of wooden steps, climbing to a crossroads of paths. Here go right to reach, within 50 yards, a stone cross, erected at a lovely spot high above another great sweep of the Hodder. Beyond it the path drops a little then runs grandly on above the river, later slanting down to approach the water's edge. Well-placed footbridges ease the way as the path emerges onto an open bank, and delightful walking leads round further bends. This is the finest section of the walk, with delectable grassy banks on which to repose. On re-entering woodland the last leg is a well-constructed path through the trees, with Higher Hodder Bridge appearing ahead. The path passes right of a house before a footbridge onto the road at the bridge.

Cromwell's Bridge

*3¾ miles from
Lower Hodder Bridge*

**Easy rambling as the Ribble
absorbs two other rivers**

*Start Junction to west
(GR: 700389), parking on
side road to Stonyhurst
Map OS Explorer 287, West Pennine Moors*

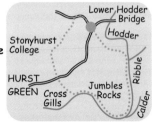

From the outset there is a fine view of Pendle Hill across the valley. From the bus shelter head up the side road for some time, largely on an overgrown footway. This levels out to approach some buildings: here take a broad driveway left to Hall Barn Farm. Don't enter the yard, but keep right on a rough road to a junction of ways. Up to the right is Stonyhurst College, visited on Walk 15. Here go straight ahead on an access track past sports fields to an old cricket pavilion. As the main track swings right to a new one, take a left branch dropping down to a gate, then along to houses at Fair Field. Turn left down their short drive onto the B6246.

Cross straight over and down the farm drive to Cross Gills, passing through to a gate/stile ahead and out on an enclosed track. From its brow this looks down on the Ribble at Jumbles, and across to Pendle Hill. The track winds down beneath a cross on a knoll, with a 19th century shaft in an older base. From the right-hand of two gates at the bottom, advance on a hedgeside to meet the Ribble. Turn left to trace the river upstream, quickly joining Jumbles farm drive: keep right on the access road past the house and continue upstream. The modest scars that break the river's flow here are known as Jumbles Rocks: enjoy also an extensive view downstream. Directly ahead appears Hacking Hall. With its imposing five gables this hoary old place dates from 1607. The fact that it stands on the opposite bank is not, at this stage, immediately apparent. Leave the drive at a kissing-gate to rejoin the bank in a lush pasture, and a great loop of the river ensues.

To your left the isolated house served by the drive is a boatman's house from when the Hacking Ferry plied the river. A small passenger boat operated into the 1950s, and an old ferry is displayed in Clitheroe's Castle Museum. The confluence of the Calder with the Ribble is reached at the first of several anglers' refuges. This idyllic spot is also a perfect vantage point for the old hall. Resume upstream, further riverside rambling leads to a track which comes in. This leads along to Winckley Hall Farm. Just prior to this a seat occupies a viewpoint overlooking the confluence of Hodder and Ribble. While the latter turns away with the Big End of Pendle directly behind, the lovely Hodder now glides quietly alongside. With the Hodder immediately hidden, turn left into the farmyard. Little remains of the house's Elizabethan origins, though some old windows hide round the back. Turn right opposite the house and out past an L-shaped pond, the remains of a moat.

Rise up the drive past the grounds of Winckley Hall, then from a kissing-gate on the right cross the field to another. A larger field is crossed towards trees on the right, from where continue along the fieldside. Part way along, on the brow, the cupolas of Stonyhurst are seen rising across the fields. From the stile at the end two short fieldsides lead past a tree-filled pond to a stile back onto the B6246. Cross with care to the junction at the start.

By the Ribble at Jumbles Rocks

*3¾ miles
from Hurst Green*

**A charming riverbank
approach to a magnificently
elegant landscape**

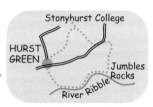

Start Village centre (GR: 685379), roadside parking
Map OS Explorer 287, West Pennine Moors

Hurst Green is a pleasant village around a wide junction, with three pubs and WCs. There is a war memorial on the green, while across the road is a Boer War memorial. The little church of St John the Evangelist dates from 1838. From the war memorial, cross the main road and turn into the car park of the Shireburn Arms: this recalls the family that owned Stonyhurst, with which the village is indelibly linked. Descend to a gate/stile and down the field with a hedge on the right: views over the valley feature Pendle Hill and Whalley Nab. When the fence turns off right, cross the fledgling stream and resume on a well-defined tongue between miniature streams. From a stile at the bottom a path passes through a few trees, then bear left outside the wood to a stile at the end. The path descends left through woodland to a bridge over a sidestream. Beyond this the riverbank is gained, and the Ribble followed upstream. At once the arches of an aqueduct are passed.

Joining Jumbles farm drive, leave the river and turn left on it, through the fields to a site of light industry at Fox Fields. Remain on the drive right into woodland. Reaching a lodge, take a gate/stile on the left and ascend the field with a tree-lined stream to its demise just short of the top. Just ahead a stile hides in the fence. Joining the B6243 turn briefly left on its footway, then cross to a gate/stile from where a hedgeside track rises away, passing New Barn to become enclosed and firmer to rise to a track junction alongside Hall Barn Farm: note the splendid barn on the right. Advance straight up the road ahead to approach Stonyhurst College. Just before the wood on the left a gate is your route of departure, but first advance a little further to savour the delights of the college. First sighting is the chapel, with the South front just to the right. Ahead are the West front and the ponds.

In its beautiful setting Stonyhurst College has long been a leading Roman Catholic boys' schools: it now takes girls too. This impressive facade is a blend of old and not so old. The original house began in the late 14th century: the Elizabethan manor house was started by Sir Richard Shireburn, and the gatehouse dates from 1592. The family line was lost in 1717, and it was handed to the Society of Jesus in 1794. 19th century extensions include the West front at the old gatehouse. St Peter's church was built in 1832-35. Facing the West front are two serene ponds beloved of waterfowl, flanking St Nicholas' Avenue created between 1690 and 1717. The school is open to visitors on afternoons in the Summer holidays, though the only Monday is at Bank Holiday. The gardens are open from earlier in July. There is a tearoom and gift shop.

Back at the gate head off along a long, narrow field, transferring to the wooded side and curving round past the end of the wood to a kissing-gate. Advance to the next such gate, then at the third, don't pass through but follow the hedge away left. At a wall follow it left through a kissing-gate and around to a gate/stile onto the head of a rough lane. Just beyond, it broadens to emerge into the village centre.

Stonyhurst College

4 miles from Hurst Green

**Rural rambling featuring
two fine old houses**

Start *Village centre*
(GR: 685379), roadside parking
Map *OS Explorer 287, West Pennine Moors*

Huntingdon
Hall
Greengore
Lane
Ends
Hud Lee
Doe Hill
HURST GREEN

For a note on Hurst Green see page 36. From the war memorial opposite the Shireburn Arms head along Avenue Road. At the Bayley Arms advance a few yards further to the see the impressive Shireburn Almshouse, with arms, inscriptions and fine semi-circular steps. From the pub, meanwhile, a sign points down a drive on the left. Pass right of garages at the bottom, and a woodland path runs on to another drive: drop to the house and pass right on a path re-entering woodland. With Dean Brook for company a broader path is joined, and the ensuing stage is a wonderful walk amid woodland and water scenery. Stone-arched Sandy Bridge leads over the beck: note the waterslides upstream. The way then rises left, out along the top of the trees into open surrounds. Ahead is the long line of Longridge Fell plastered in conifers. This green way rises delightfully between enclosing greenery, merging into a drive rising to Greengore. Its intriguing architecture includes novel buttresses: dating back several centuries it was once a hunting lodge.

Keep straight on, right of the buildings, and as the track fades a good path continues up the wallside outside the wood. The path runs on beyond the wood through colourful surrounds, along the edge of a new plantation on the left. From the gate at the end ignore the fork of tracks for a thin path slanting up rough pasture, aiming for a skyline ladder-stile between clumps of trees. Look back over richly-wooded country to the cupolas of Stonyhurst, with Pendle Hill beyond. Head away above the wood on your left, on beneath a gorse bank to be deflected right alongside a new hedge. With views over the Ribble to the West Pennine Moors, this leads all the way on to a gate/stile at the end to join a road.

Turn left to descend past Huntingdon Hall, a superb old house of 1619, and down to houses at Lane Ends, where turn left on Carlinghurst drive. In the yard pass two houses, and with a third ahead, use a gate set back between barns on the left. A track heads across a field to a gate on the brow: as it swings right take a stile in front, and bear left to another in the facing hedge. Cross towards Higher Hud Lee, bearing right onto its drive. Follow this right the short way to the buildings at Lower Hud Lee. Go left on the short access road, and along the front of the second house to a wall-stile at the end. A short-lived green way leads to a gate/stile into a field. Slant gently right across this large pasture, crossing a moist ditch, then a second one at a pond. Cross to the right edge of a wood where stile and footbridge put you into a meadow. Bear right across the centre, bound for tree-capped Doe Hill.

Over a footbridge rise to a stile out of the meadow and left of the trees on beneath an Ordnance Survey column: at just 472ft/144m this enjoys big views, notably to Longridge Fell across fields and scattered woodland. On the brow just past it locate a stile in the hedge onto an access road at New House. Go right, dropping gently to a junction with a back road. Turn left, dropping to cross Dean Brook on the village edge. The road rises back into the centre, though you might finish by a path up the scrubby bank on the right, rising through trees to become enclosed by gardens back out onto the road almost opposite the Shireburn Arms.

Huntingdon Hall

4¹4 miles from Salesbury

Easy rambling through beautiful riverside scenery

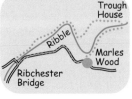

Start **Marles Wood (GR: 675356), car park near Salesbury Hall east of Ribchester Bridge**
Map OS Explorer 287, West Pennine Moors

A little path from the car park short-cuts the drive to join the road. Descend the road through the wood, quickly levelling out to wind on past zealous modern developments at Salesbury Hall to arrive via a large house at Ribchester Bridge. On the left is the former De Tabley inn, recalling an important land-owning family. Two minutes further is New Hall, a fine 17th century house with mullioned windows and a carving above the doorway.

Ribchester Bridge with its three graceful arches dates from 1774. Cross with care and turn upstream on a farm drive: far ahead is Pendle Hill. The drive leaves the river part way along to reach Dewhurst House. Entering the yard, turn down to the right to find a short-lived path meeting the riverbank in a lovely setting. The grassy path turns upstream, staying generally close to the river. Passing beneath Stewart's Wood the main path forks left up the bank, dropping back to enter Haugh Wood at a stile/footbridge. A glorious woodland section ensues on the bank, which here undertakes a great sweep. Just before the end the path swings up to the left to a stile out of the trees, and climbs the small bank into a field. Cross the centre of this extensive pasture which could be almost anywhere. On the brow you are greeted by a super panorama, with a sweep of the river leading the eye to Pendle Hill. Drop left to a gate/stile in a dip, then bear left across the pasture, soon swinging uphill to a gate/stile at the far corner. Slant up across a small enclosure to a bridle-gate onto a driveway above Hey Hurst.

A few steps down the drive, a bridle-gate opposite sends you off down a hedgeside, meeting a wood at the end to descend outside it to a footbridge at the bottom. From it follow a hedge away, along the bottoms of several fields until a fence parts company. With the supports of the Dinckley footbridge appearing over to the right, keep straight on to a gate ahead, a track becoming enclosed to pass through a strip plantation. Emerging just before Trough House Farm, leave the track on a short, enclosed path doubling back to the bridge. Cross in style on this high suspension bridge, enjoying lovely views both up and down river. The far bank is the place to take in the verdant loveliness: the bridge was erected in 1951, replacing a ferry. Just beneath the bridge a series of scars interrupt the water's flow, while herons are regularly sighted.

Turn downstream to enjoy the walk's loveliest section, with fine woodland increasingly encroaching. An intervening pasture is crossed with the river partly obscured by trees, but at the other end a smashing prospect is revealed as the Ribble glides between richly wooded banks. A kissing-gate admits to Marles Wood, and a gem of a path heads away above the river. At the far end the rocks of Coppy Scar call for a further halt. This aggressively attractive section of river features the whirlpool of Sale Wheel, before it turns away for contrastingly lazy sweeps. Your path bears left to remain in the trees, and an early concessionary path climbs directly to the car park. Alternatively, remain on the right of way which, beyond a footbridge, itself climbs onto the road below the car park.

The Ribble at Sale Wheel

4$\frac{1}{2}$ miles from Ribchester

Old dewponds scattered by fieldpaths above a Roman site

Start Village centre (GR: 650350), car park Map OS Explorer 287, West Pennine Moors

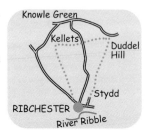

Ribchester Roman fort guarded a river crossing on a road north from Manchester: the Roman Museum has a copy of a helmet found by the river. St Wilfrid's church has a 14th century tower, Jacobean pulpit and 1735 box pews. Along with the Black Bull pub is the White Bull of 1707, its columns claimed as Roman. There is a tearoom and a Post office/shop. From the end of the main street above the river a path goes left past the school, with an immediate prospect of the wide-flowing Ribble. The path leads to the Roman bath-house, then over a bridge and a green space onto a back road, Greenside. Turn right to a junction opposite the Ribchester Arms, and right past it then left up Stydd Lane. This rises past a school to a fascinating corner. Here is St Peter & St Paul's Catholic church of 1789 and Stydd Almshouses, built in 1728 by the Shireburns of Stonyhurst. Continue up the drive to 12th century St Saviours' church, with Norman windows and doorway: an old cross base is out front.

The drive ends at a farm, Stydd Manor. Head up the yard, emerging via two gates into a field. A track rises away with a hedge on the right. At the top corner the track goes through a gate, but take a stile alongside. Resume with a hedge on the left to a footbridge at the top. Ascend another large pasture to a gate/stile at the top. On the left is a dry dewpond: made to quench cattle's thirst, it is the first of many. Higher to the left is a mast. The climb ends by way of a sunken way on the brow. At 410ft/125m this high point on Duddel Hill gives views to Longridge Fell ahead and Pendle Hill to the right: behind is the Ribble Valley backed by the West Pennine Moors. The part-sunken way runs to a farmhouse. Through a gate to its left follow the drive out to the B6243: without joining, go left across the field to a stile, continuing to another across a large field. As it falls away at the end, drop to a footbridge on Stydd Brook. A thin path slants up the opposite bank, crossing a tiny sidestream and then left, outside a garden at Cox Farm to a stile onto a road.

Go briefly right to a stile on the left, and cross the field to a stile in a hedge right of an old dewpond. Continue through a gateway in a hedge, then bear right to a corner stile. Head away with a scant hedge on the left, past a former dewpond to another corner stile. Cross a large field centre to the end of a row of trees on the right, a track forming to join a firmer one with Kellets Farm to the right. Go left on this drive to a house. Pass through a gate/stile ahead and bear right across the field past an old dewpond to a stile into a wooded gill. A path drops to a footbridge, then bear right up the other side to a gate/stile at the top. A faint fenceside track heads away, a line that will be maintained on this steady descent.

Through a gate/stile at the bottom drop to merge with a ditch, crossing to a stile then resuming across to another at a tree-lined stream. Rise away to resume past another old pond, remaining with the left-hand boundary to curve right, down past another to cross an old access track near the bottom. From a gate/stile below, pass through another ahead and then through a longer pasture to its tapering end. Here cross a bridge and go right on the track to a gate at the edge of housing where it runs enclosed out onto a road on the edge of the village. Go left to finish. *Stydd Almshouses*

4 miles from Knowle Green

Easy rambling onto a tract of colourful moorland

Start New Row (GR: 648381),
*parking a short mile east
on Hurst Green road*
Map OS Explorer 287, West Pennine Moors

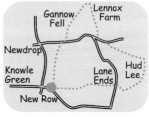

By seats and a postbox a drive heads away from the road:
your start instead bears right along the front of the whitewashed
cottages of New Row. At the end a path drops to a gate onto an
access road: go left to a new house and on to a gate beyond. Cross
to the right end of a plantation, over a stile just before it then along
the fieldside outside the trees. At the end drop to a kissing-gate
into trees, emerging onto a drive. Go left to bridge Duddel Brook
and within 25 yards the path resumes on the right, rising through
trees to a stile into a field. Head away, rising left to a corner stile,
and on again to one opposite before crossing to a house. A stile onto
the lawn sends you left of the house and onto a road at Lane Ends.
    Just a few yards left take the drive to Carlinghurst. In
the yard pass two houses, and with a third ahead, take a gate set
back between barns on the left. A track heads away across a field
to a gate on the brow. As the track swings right take a stile in front,
and bear left to another in the facing hedge. Cross towards Higher
Hud Lee, taking a gate/stile into Hudd Lee Wood just left of the
farm. A path rises away right, then levels out to run to a bridle-gate at
the end. A track passes between new plantings, then drops right to a
junction at the plantation corner. Double back left on a path slanting
up the rough pasture to a skyline ladder-stile between clumps of trees:
look back over richly-wooded country to Pendle Hill. Slant up again to
a brow revealing Longridge Fell's western half. Maintain this line to
the right-hand of two corners, slanting slightly down to a stile. Now
slant up a smaller pasture to a gate/stile onto Old Clitheroe Road, a
good place to survey a skyline from Pendle to the West Pennine Moors.

Go left to the start of woods and turn right up an access road. This rises past a cottage of 1842, emerging above the wood on the left with views over Gannow Fell. Approaching Lennox Farm on the left, use a gate to cross the field beneath it, at 820ft/250m the walk's high point. Across a stream beneath the house continue across to find a stile onto the open moor of Gannow Fell: in front is a recolonised quarry. A thin trod bears left, rising gently through bracken and heather on traces of old quarry track before slanting down across the moor. The charming little path remains on the line of the old track through heather and bilberry as it drops beneath an old reservoir to a gate back onto Old Clitheroe Road.

Go briefly right past Hougher Fall Farm then take a stile on the left. Through a gate at the bottom of this small enclosure go right on a short track to a modern barn. Before it, drop left to a gate below, most likely with poultry in attendance! Turn right with fence and tree-lined stream to a small gate in the bottom corner. Advancing briefly on, take a stile into the corner of the wood for a few strides only to a stile out of the corner. Ahead are extensive lower Ribble views. Resume with the tiny stream, the fence quickly turning off as you maintain the slant through colourful pasture. Pass through sheep pens at the bottom and over the stream to resume down to a gate/stile on the other side. Now bear right across the field to a gate/stile in the far corner. Go left down an enclosed green way to Squire House. Continue down the drive onto the road.

Old reservoir, Gannow Fell

4 miles
from Jeffrey Hill

Easy moorland walking with
majestic views to Bowland

Start Cardwell House (GR:
639401), car park on road top
Map OS Explorer OL41, Forest of Bowland & Ribblesdale
Access Open access, see page 5

Before even pulling your boots on, you will be stunned by the views across Chipping's fertile vale to the Bowland fells. From a kissing-gate at the top of the parking area a broad path heads away to rise gently through reedy pasture. A stone waymark sends it left at a fork, commencing a level stride past another and above a steeper drop, on through heather to a waymark at a path junction by a tiny stream. Go right on the main path rising alongside a reedy tract, easing out to give the walk's only view south, with Winter Hill dominant. It runs to a wall at a plantation corner: don't pass through but rise up the wallside through heather, crossing a fence-stile where the Ordnance Survey column is revealed ahead. Before it however a cross-path is met alongside a stile/bridle-gate: to this you will return after the short detour to the summit, straight ahead.

The OS column stands at 1148ft/350m on the top known as Spire Hill. For such a modest height Longridge offers a remarkable panorama. Its detachment from other high ground is the key, allied to the fact that the Bowland massif is so near, its moors arrayed in total splendour. From Beacon Fell round to Waddington Fell, the wonderful heights of Parlick, Fair Snape and Totridge front this upland dome. Its foreground complements it, with the wooded Hodder gliding through green fields liberally scattered with farms. The village of Chipping is evident towards the foot of Parlick. Further back are some of the peaks of the Yorkshire Dales, most notably Ingleborough and Penyghent.

On leaving, retrace steps with the wall to the path cross-roads. Turn right here on an inviting path through heather, rapidly gaining an edge to earn an appreciation of the great northern scarp of the fell. The path swings right to enjoy a superb slant down with an old sunken way. Towards the bottom, double back left on a reedy way to a gate in the wall below, leaving the fell. Bear slightly left down a large pasture, reaching a stile in the right end of a fence. Drop down a reedy corner tapering to an enclosed way, where stiles and gates lead out via sheep pens onto a road at Bradley Hall.

Turn left for a quiet half-mile to the first drive on the left, rising to Rams Clough. Pass between the houses to a gate ahead, then slant right up unkempt pasture to a corner marked by a junction of reedy boundary ditches. Rise again to escape further reeds and slant towards the next corner beneath a pronounced ditch. Just past a forlorn gatepost swing left in front of a small stream to a gate back onto the fell. An intermittent path sets off right along the base, never far above the wall. Cross the stream and negotiate a smaller one just behind, after which several moist reedy sections are encountered. During a slight height gain things improve, particularly amid heather. Above a house the wall drops away: keep straight on, angling higher to gain more level ground to leave the fell where you began.

Looking north on the descent from Longridge Fell

HILLSIDE GUIDES... cover much of Northern England

Other colour *Pocket Walks* guides (more in preparation)
·UPPER WHARFEDALE   ·LOWER WHARFEDALE
·UPPER WENSLEYDALE   ·LOWER WENSLEYDALE
·MALHAMDALE   ·SWALEDALE   ·RIBBLESDALE
·INGLETON/WESTERN DALES   ·SEDBERGH/DENTDALE
·NIDDERDALE   ·HARROGATE/KNARESBOROUGH
·BOWLAND   ·AROUND PENDLE   ·RIBBLE VALLEY
·AMBLESIDE/LANGDALE   ·BORROWDALE
·AIRE VALLEY   ·ILKLEY/WASHBURN VALLEY

Our *Walking Country* range features more great walks...

·WHARFEDALE   ·MALHAMDALE   ·WENSLEYDALE
·HARROGATE & the WHARFE VALLEY   ·SWALEDALE
·RIPON & LOWER WENSLEYDALE   ·NIDDERDALE
·THREE PEAKS ·HOWGILL FELLS · HOWARDIAN HILLS
·TEESDALE   ·EDEN VALLEY   ·ALSTON & ALLENDALE

·ILKLEY MOOR   ·BRONTE COUNTRY   ·CALDERDALE
·PENDLE & the RIBBLE   ·WEST PENNINE MOORS
·ARNSIDE & SILVERDALE   ·LUNESDALE   ·BOWLAND

·LAKELAND FELLS, SOUTH   ·LAKELAND FELLS, EAST
·LAKELAND FELLS, NORTH   ·LAKELAND FELLS, WEST

Long Distance Walks
·COAST TO COAST WALK ·CUMBRIA WAY ·DALES WAY
·LADY ANNE'S WAY   ·NIDDERDALE WAY
·WESTMORLAND WAY   ·FURNESS WAY
·PENDLE WAY   ·BRONTE WAY   ·CALDERDALE WAY

Visit www.hillsidepublications.co.uk
or write for a catalogue